Penguin Poetry
CANAAN

Geoffrey Hill was born in 1932 at Bromsgrove, Worcestershire, where his father was a police constable. He attended Fairfield Junior School, the County High School, Bromsgrove, and Keble College, Oxford (which elected him into an honorary fellowship in 1981). He taught for many years at Leeds University, later at Cambridge, where he is an Honorary Fellow of Emmanuel College. In 1988 he moved to the USA and is a member of the University Professors Program at Boston University. He is the author of six books of poetry and two collections of critical essays, and his *Collected Poems* is published in the Penguin International Poets series. His version of Ibsen's *Brand*, which was commissioned by the Royal National Theatre in 1978, is now published in Penguin Classics.

CANAAN

Geoffrey Hill

PENGUIN BOOKS

PENGUIN BOOKS

Published by the Penguin Group
Penguin Books Ltd, 27 Wrights Lane, London w8 5tz, England
Penguin Books USA Inc., 375 Hudson Street, New York, New York 10014, USA
Penguin Books Australia Ltd, Ringwood, Victoria, Australia
Penguin Books Canada Ltd, 10 Alcorn Avenue, Toronto, Ontario, Canada M4V 3B2
Penguin Books (NZ) Ltd, 182–190 Wairau Road, Auckland 10, New Zealand

Penguin Books Ltd, Registered Offices: Harmondsworth, Middlesex, England

This collection first published in 1996

10 9 8 7 6 5 4 3 2 1

Set in 10.5/15 pt Monotype Bembo
Designed in QuarkXpress on an Apple Macintosh
Printed in England by Clays Ltd, St Ives plc

ENL (PO)
L52739N

In memory of Jack Hallas

... So $\overset{e}{y}$ children of Israél did wickedly in the sight of the Lord, & forgate the Lord their God, & serued Baalím, and Asheróth ... Yea, they offred their sonnes, and their daughters vnto diuels, And shed innocent blood, euen the blood of their sonnes, and of their daughters, whome they offred vnto the idols of Canáan, and the land was defiled with blood. Thus were they steined with their owne workes, and went a whoring with their owne inuentions ... ô Canáan, the land of the Philistims, I wil euen destroy thee without an inhabitant.

Judges 3:7; Psalm 106: 37–9; Zephaniah 2:5
(from the Geneva Bible of 1560)

CONTENTS

TO THE HIGH COURT OF PARLIAMENT
November 1994

Where's probity in this –
                the slither-frisk
to lordship of a kind
as rats to a bird-table?

England – now of genius
                the eidolon –
unsubstantial yet voiding
substance like quicklime:

privatize to the dead
her memory:
                let her wounds weep
into the lens of oblivion.

THAT MAN AS A RATIONAL ANIMAL DESIRES THE KNOWLEDGE WHICH IS HIS PERFECTION

Abiding provenance I would have said
the question stands
                          even in adoration
clause upon clause
                          with or without assent
reason and desire on the same loop –
I imagine singing I imagine

getting it right – the knowledge
of sensuous intelligence
                    entering into the work –
spontaneous happiness as it was once
given our sleeping nature to awake by
                                    and know
innocence of first inscription

SOBIESKI'S SHIELD

I

The blackberry, white
field-rose, all others
of that family:

steadfast is the word

and the star-gazing planet out of which
lamentation is spun.

2

Brusque as the year
        purple garish-brown
aster chrysanthemum
        signally restored
to a subsistence of slant light
as one might assert
            Justice Equity
or Sobieski's Shield even
            the names
and what they have about them dark to dark.

OF COMING INTO BEING
AND PASSING AWAY
To Aileen Ireland

Rosa sericea: its red
spurs
    blooded with amber
each lit and holy grain
the sun
      makes much of
as of all our shadows –

prodigal ever returning
darkness that in such circuits
reflects diuturnity
        to itself
and to our selves
        yields nothing
finally –

    but by occasion
visions of truth or dreams
as they arise –
      to terms of grace
where grace has surprised us –
the unsustaining
        wondrously sustained

DE ANIMA

Salutation: it is as though
effortlessly — to reprise —
                    the unsung spirit
gestures of no account
become accountable
                         such matters arising
whatever it is that is sought

                    through metaphysics
research into angelic song
ending as praise itself
the absolute yet again
atoned with the contingent —
                              typology
incarnate — Bethlehem the open field —

still to conceive no otherwise: an
aphasia of staring wisdom
the souls images glassily exposed
                    fading to silverpoint
still to be at the last
ourselves and masters of all
                         humility —

WHETHER THE VIRTUES
ARE EMOTIONS

Overnight – overnight –
                          the inmost
self made outcast: here
plighting annihilations
                          unfinished
business of eros
                the common numen

of waking
          reverie where you had dreamt
to be absolved:
                  and with the day
forsakenness
            the new bride brought forth:
carnal desuetude

her mystic equity
her natures ripped hardihood
the radiant
            windrows where a storm
emptied its creels
thrusting ailanthus that is called
                  the Tree of Heaven

WHETHER MORAL VIRTUE COMES
BY HABITUATION

It is said that sometimes even fear
drops away –
            exhausted – I would not
deny that: self
expression – you could argue – the first to go –
immolated
        selfhood the last:

deprivation therefore
              dereliction even
become the things we rise to:
ethereal conjecture
           taking on
humankinds heaviness of purchase
the moral nebulae

          common as lichen
the entire corpus of ruinous sagesse
moved by some rite
         and pace of being
as by earth in her slow
           approaches to withdrawal
the processionals of seared array

RITORNELLI
For Hugh Wood on his 60th Birthday

i

Angel of Tones
                  flame of accord
exacting mercies
                      answerable
to rage as solace

I will have you sing

ii

For so the judgement
passes
      it is not
otherwise
          hereafter
you will see them resolved
in tears
        they shall bear
your crowns of redress

iii

Lost to no thought
of triumph he returns
upon himself goes down
among water and ash
and wailing sounds confused
with sounds of joy

TO WILLIAM COBBETT: IN ABSENTIA

I say it is not faithless
to stand without faith, keeping open
vigil at the site.
Who shall endure? What force throws off
the verdict of each day's
idle and taunting honours,
the lottery, the trade in grief,
the outrageous quittance, the shiftless
orders of fools?
I say let stand the entire
deposed authority
of vision just as it fell;
your righteous unjust and cordial anger,
your singular pitch where labour is spoken of,
your labour that brought to pass
reborn Commodity with uplifted hands
awed by its own predation.

CANAAN

I

They march at God's
pleasure through Flanders
with machine-pistols,
chorales, cannon
of obese bronze,
with groaning pushcarts,
to topple Baal. At
crossroads they hoist
corpses and soiled
banners of the Lamb.
The sun takes assize.
Aloof the blades
of oblation
rise, fall, as though they
were not obstructed
by blades of bone.

Fourier's children
their steeds, kazoos,
the splashed fetlocks –
deliquescent manna
that most resembles
a sudden urban sleet –
shedding innocent blood
their ragged fusillade
a bit of a laugh
indifferent hatred
stained with their own works:
détentes of corpse-gas
                     reactive
furnaces of the spirit
immemorial
           sightings in Canaan:
fig trees and planted vines
and the groves
                unguarded
messuage for jackals.

III

Iniquity passes
and rectitude.
They do not spare
the sucking child nor are they
sparing with trumpets.
Now it is
Moloch his ovens
and the dropped babes naked
swung by an arm
or a leg like flails.

DARK-LAND

Aspiring Grantham
rises above itself.
Tall churches wade the fen
on their stilts of glass.

Crowned Ely stands beset
by winds of straw-burning,
by the crouched run of flame.
Cambridge lies dark, and dead

predestined Elstow
where Bunyan struck his fear –
flint creed, tinder of wrath –
to flagrant mercies.

MYSTICISM AND DEMOCRACY

Open me the gates of righteousness: That I may go into them

You see the terrain he has won back from but not won;
the ravaged moon is a mere cranium, a mandarin crown,
                      compared to these craters.
He is indeed a survivor and of the intolerable elect.
Enforce for jollity's sake a solemn retaking
of the earth that has been his, many times over, by deed.
Project through lanterns of hot oil the festive advance –
                      it is at once a retreat
to that furthest point where lines of vanishing converge.
The obscurities through which you have armed his way,
night marches, down-draughts of coal smoke,
                      many-chambered fog lit from within,
become to hurled applause: the Veil of the Nations, the Final
Transformation-Scene-and-Curtain, Apocalypse-Hippodrome!

SCENES WITH HARLEQUINS

In memoriam Aleksandr Blok

*Joyfully I accept this strange book, joyfully and with fear
— in it there is so much beauty, poetry, death. I await the
accomplishment of your task* — Volokhova to Blok, 1907

*All the sounds have gone silent. Can't you hear that there
aren't any sounds any more?* — Blok, 1920

I

Distance is on edge;
the level tide
stands rimmed with mercury.
Again the estranged spirit

is possessed of light.
The common things
glitter uncommonly.
City besieged by the sun

amid sybilline
galas, a dust
pluming the chariots
of tyrants and invalids,

peppered with mica,
granite-faced seer
scathed by invisible
planets as men dream of war

like a fresh sea-wind
like the lilac
at your petrified heart
as something anciently known ...

II

The day preens, the birds
gust from the square.
Ferrous sulphate
vapours in the dens

of dead photographers.
With white seraphic
hair against the sun
who are these strangers –

or who are these
charred spirits glaring
their vitreous eyes
towards apocalypse?

They are not of our flesh
to do them justice.
Still they outshine us
among the prophets.

III

Beautiful Lady,
with reverence
in sorrow in masquerade,
how else should we have lived?

Tempestuous fantasies,
blood-tinted opaline
essential clouds,
I am not myself

I think in this last act
without end. Lordly
and faithful servant of Life –
what can one say?

By humour of lament,
spontaneous word of stone,
inspired débâcle
many times rehearsed,

look to abide
tyrannous egality
and freedom led forth
blinded by prophecies.

Now it is gleeting Venus
who so decrees and now
it is parched Mars,
Beautiful Lady.

IV

The risen Christ! Once more
faith is upon us,
a jubilant brief keening
without respite:

Obedience, bitter joy,
the elements, clouds,
winds, louvres where the bell
makes its wild mouths:

Holy Rus – into the rain's
horizons, peacock-dyed
tail-feathers of storm,
so it goes on.

V

Even now one is amazed
by transience: how it
outlasts us all.
Motley of shadow

dabbles the earth,
the malachite-pocked
nymphs and sea gods, the pear tree's
motionless wooden leaves.

In this light, constrained spirit,
be a lord of your age.
Rejoice; let the strange
legends begin.

VI

Of Rumor, of Clamor,
I shall be silent;
I will not deal
in the vatic exchanges

between committees,
mysticism by the book.
History is adorned
with bookish fires.

Begone you grave jewellers
and you spartan hoplites
in masks of foil.
Orthodox arcane

interpreters of repute,
this is understood.
Why should I hear
further what you propose?

Exegetes may come
to speak to the silence
that has arisen. It is
not unheard of.

VII

Decembrist blood! We are taxed
for their visions. The earth
turns, returns, through cycles
of declamation;

with feuilletons and iron
fantasies of the state.
Rhadamanthine the grim
torches of naphtha,

the unspeakable dull woe
of which I may have had
foreknowledge – I forget –
in 'Retribution'.

POSTLUDE

Rose-douched ammoniac
arch goddess
of intimate apparel,
brutal and bijou,

regarding the sensual
imperative despair,
see: there are worse times,
this blank platz,

the bronze humps
of Gaea and Kronos;
spates of fat snow-melt
swallow their parturitions.

ALGABAL
Stefan George, 1868–1933

Rhine-rentier,
contemptuous bankrupt,
you placed sacraments
in the hands of receivers.

Contempt is in order: one
                would give much
to see those Frankish
rites nobly concluded.

Almost, for Childe Stauffenberg,
it fell so;
but this was tragedy
botched, unimagined,

within that circle.
Medallion-profile
                    of hauteur,
Caesarian abstinence!

Your desk is a pure altar;
                it is not
for the coarse earthen things
to bleed their spirit;

but for a vital
scintillant atrophy,
a trophy
of the ageless champion.

MYSTICISM AND DEMOCRACY

i

Do not stand witness; observe only
natures and polities aligned with rectitude
                    yet not of it;
commonweal their lodestar, inordinate
and thrusting dominion their enterprise;
purposed ambition not to be confined
                    by reason of defect.

ii

To some, self-found, defected, secret resources,
tacit amnesties beyond denial,
like botanists' or scholars' chance marginalia,
certain debts of trust
                    in commendation.
There being now such riotous shows of justice,
yet, of righteousness, the fading nimbus
remains to us, as a perceived glory.

iii

Is it then by default that we do not
stoop to their honours? It is not wholly true
that what the world commands is a lesser thing.
Who shall restore the way, reclaim lost footage,
achieve too late prescient telegraphy,
take to themselves otherness of common woe,
devotion bought from abeyance,
                    fortitude to be held
at the mercy of door-chimes?

DARK-LAND

Wherein Wesley stood
up from his father's grave,
summoned familiar dust
for strange salvation:

whereto England rous'd,
ignorant, her inane
Midas-like hunger: smoke
engrossed, cloud-cumbered,

a spectral people
raking among the ash;
its freedom a lost haul
of entailed riches.

How swiftly they cease to be
incredible
          how incredible
the sudden immortals –

a tilt   a flare
as though of mirrors –

dared by their luck
they outdare it
               and spin
from the fumy towers
taking England with them –
flame-tattered
                    pirouettes
quenched in a cloud.

PARENTALIA

The here-and-now finds vigil transfiguring
whatever is
          yet ignorant of your beauty.
Any one of us, given a certain light,
          shall make and be immortal:
streets of Jerusalem, seraphs the passers-by,
and other extras, artisans per diem,
imperative in hindsight
          a brief blessing.
I cannot tell how we might be otherwise
drawn to the things occluded, manifold,
the measureless that stands
          even so depleted
in the faint rasp of dry autumnal flowers.

RESPUBLICA

PARENTALIA

The strident high
civic trumpeting
of misrule. It is
what we stand for.

Wild insolence,
aggregates without
distinction. Courage
of common men:

spent in the ruck
their remnant witness
after centuries
is granted them

like a pardon.
And other fealties
other fortitudes
broken as named —

Respublica
brokenly recalled,
its archaic laws
and hymnody;

and destroyed hope
that so many times
is brought with triumph
back from the dead.

DE JURE BELLI AC PACIS

i.m. Hans-Bernd von Haeften, 1905–1944

I

The people moves as one spirit unfettered
claim our assessors of stone.

                    When the nations
fall dispossessed such conjurings possess them,
elaborate barren fountains, projected
aqueducts

          where water is no longer found.
Where would one find Grotius for that matter,
the secular justice clamant among psalms,
huge-fisted visionary Comenius ... ?
Could none predict these haughty degradations
as now your high-strung

                   martyred resistance serves
to consecrate the liberties of Maastricht?

... sah er den Erzengel Michael im Kampf gegen den Drachen,
Michael, den Engel der deutschen Geschichte ...

The iron-beamed engine-shed has chapel windows.
Glare-eyed, you spun. The hooks are still in the beam;
a sun-patch drains to nothing; here the chocked
blade sluiced into place, here the abused blood
                              set its own wreaths.
Time passes, strengthening and fading. Europa
hetaera displays her parts, her triumph
to tax even Dürer's resplendent economy
in rictus and graven sorrow.
                              On some envisioned
rathaus clock, geared like a mill, the dragon
strikes,
        the Archangel, unseeing, unbowed,
chimes with each stroke.

III

You foretold us, hazarding the proscribed tongue
of piety and shame; plain righteousness
committed with much else to Kreisau's bees
for their particular keeping. We might have kept
your Christian inhibitions – faithful, non-jurant,
in the singing-court of dread
                       at the grid of extortion –
but chose pity. This pity is shameless
unlike memory, though both can draw
sugar from iron.
                Pity, alone with its rage,
settles on multitudes
                  as the phoenix sought
from a hundred cities tribute of requiting flame.

IV

In Plötzensee where you were hanged

                            they now hang
tokens of reparation and in good faith
compound with Cicero's maxims, Schiller's chant,
your silenced verities.

                    To the high-minded
base-metal forgers of this common Europe,
community of parody, you stand ec-
centric as a prophet. There is no better
vision that I can summon: you were upheld
on the strong wings of the Psalms before you died.
Evil is not good's absence but gravity's
everlasting bedrock and its fatal chains
inert, violent, the suffrage of our days.

V

Not harmonies – harmonics, astral whisperings
light-years above the stave; groans, murmurs, cries,
tappings from cell to cell. It is a night-watch,
indeterminate and of vast concentration,
of those redeeming their pledged fear, who strike
faith from the hard rock of God's fallenness;
their pain draws recompense beyond our grasp
of recapitulation.
          Slurred clangour,
cavernous and chained haltings, echo from time's
inchoate music, the theme standing proclaimed
only in the final measures –
                      Vexilla regis
uplifted by Rüdiger Schleicher's violin.

VI

*der Tod ... nahm über uns Gewalt,
Hielt uns in seinem Reich gefangen.
Hallelujah!*

Those three eternal days Christus did not lie
shackled in death:
                    but found out your stark reich,
deep-buried hypocausts dense for the harrowing,
held there – since time so holds within itself –
slow precise Fellgiebel, chivalrous Hofacker,
clamped in their silence:
                    keeps also Goerdeler's
doubled, many-times-consummated, agony:
in whatever fortress, on whatever foundation,
then, now, in eternum, the spirit bears witness
                    through its broken flesh:
to grace more enduring even than mortal corruption,
ineradicable, and rightly so.

VII

Smart whip-tap at boot-top, absolute
                    licence of the demons
to wreak their correction; elsewhere they are fixed
self-torches in sulphur; as there is a God,
                    elsewhere, of jealous mercy
this is not news: the book of Daniel's strength
unwritten, Zion's resurgent lamentation
in Kreisau's witnessing here undenizened
to the sand, to the old waste.
                    So let the rights
be speculation, fantastic pickings, late
                    gold of Europa
in her brief modish rags –
                    Schindler! Schindler!

VIII

Hinrichtungsstätte war ein Schuppen im Gefängnis ...

But if – but if; and if nowhere
                              but here
archives for catacombs; letters, codes, prayers,
film-scraps, dossiers, shale of crunched shellac,
new depths of invention, children's
                              songs to mask torture ...
Christus, it is not your stable: it will serve
as well as any other den or shippen
the arraigned truth, the chorus with its gifts
of humiliation, incense and fumitory,
                              Lucerna,
the soul-flame, as it has stood through such ages,
ebbing, and again, lambent, replenished,
                              in its stoup of clay.

CYCLE
William Arrowsmith, 1924–1992

1

Natural strange beatitudes
                                    the leafless tints
of spring touch red through brimstone
what do you mean   praise and lament
it is the willow
                    first then
larch or alder

2

The heart feels for its own
                                    patience
reflects upon itself
light is everywhere
                            the spiders'
galaxies
            droppings of the
star wormwood

3

So there   there it is   past
reason and measure
                            sustaining
the constancy of mischance
its occlusion
                    a spasm
a psalm

4

Are we not moved by
                    'savage
indignation' or whatever
strange
        natürlich
dance with antlers
paces over and
                over the same
ground

5

Larch or alder
                first
then willow
            leafless tints
of spring touch red through brimstone

praise and lament
praise and lament

what do you mean
                    praise
lament
        praise and lament
what do you mean
                    do you mean
beatitudes

SORREL

Very common and widely distributed . . . It is called Sorrow . . .
in some parts of Worcestershire.

Memory worsening – let it go as rain
streams on half-visible clatter of the wind
                    lapsing and rising,
that clouds the pond's green mistletoe of spawn,
seeps among nettlebeds and rust-brown sorrel,
perpetual ivy burrowed by weak light,
makes carved shapes crumble: the ill-weathering stone
salvation's troth-plight, plumed, of the elect.

PARENTALIA
Daniel 12:3–4, 9

Go your ways, as if in thanksgiving:
Daniel finally instructed of the Lord.
The book is closed for your time; it will not
          open again to the slow
round of the psalms, the prophets of righteousness.
But go, as instrumental, of the Lord,
          life-bound to his foreknowledge
and in his absence making your return
to the generations, the rosaceae,
the things of earth snagging the things of grace,
darkened hawthorn, its late flare, that stands
illustrious, and the darkening season –
Harvest Festival to Armistice Day
          the other harvest.

MYSTICISM AND DEMOCRACY

I am of Dark-land, for there I was born, and there my Father and Mother are still.

To the Evangelicals: a moving image
of multitudes turned aside –
                              into the fields –
with staves and bundles, through the patched sloughs,
broken-down hedges, among brick stacks:
unerring the voice, the direction, though the truth
                              is difficult to follow,
a track of peculiar virtue – English – which so often
                              deceives us by the way.
Exhaustion is of the essence, though in the meantime
what song has befallen those who were laggard
pilgrims, or none. It is as you see. I would not
trouble greatly to proclaim this.
                              But shelve it under Mercies.

CHURCHILL'S FUNERAL

I

... one dark day in the Guildhall: looking at the memorials of the city's
great past & knowing well the history of its unending charity, I seemed to
hear far away in the dim roof a theme, an echo of some noble melody ...

Endless London
mourns for that knowledge
under the dim roofs
of smoke-stained glass,

the men hefting
their accoutrements
of webbed tin, many
in bandages,

with cigarettes,
with scuffed hands aflare,
as though exhaustion
drew them to life;

as if by some
miraculous draft
of enforced journeys
their peace were made

strange homecoming
into sleep, blighties,
and untouched people
among the maimed:

nobilmente it
rises from silence,
the grand tune, and goes
something like this.

II

Suppose the subject of inquiry, instead of being House-law (Oikonomia),
had been star-law (Astronomia), and that, ignoring distinction between stars
fixed and wandering, as here between wealth radiant and wealth reflective,
the writer had begun thus:

Innocent soul
ghosting for its lost
twin, the afflicted one,
born law-giver;

uncanny wraith
kindled afar-off
like the evening star,
res publica

seen by itself
with its whole shining
history discerned
through shining air,

both origin
and consequence, its
hierarchies of sorts,
fierce tea-making

in time of war,
courage and kindness
as the marvel is
the common weal

that will always,
simply as of right,
keep faith, ignorant
of right or fear:

who is to judge
who can judge of this?
Maestros of the world
not you not them.

III

Los listens to the Cry of the Poor Man; his Cloud
Over London in volume terrific low bended in anger.

The copper clouds
are not of this light;
Lambeth is no more
the house of the lamb.

The meek shall die rich
would you believe:
with such poverty
lavished upon them,

with their obsequies
the Heinkels' lourd drone
and Fame darkening
her theatres

to sirens, laughter,
the frizzed angels
of visitation
powdered by the blast,

the catafalques
like gin-palaces
where she entertains
the comedians.

IV

St Mary Abchurch, St Mary Aldermanbury, St Mary-le-Bow . . .

Stone Pietà
for which the city
offers up incense
and ashes, blitzed

firecrews, martyrs
crying to the Lord,
their mangled voices
within the flame;

to which we bring
litanies of scant
survival and all
random mercies,

with the ragwort
and the willow-herb
as edifiers
of ruined things.

V

. . . every minute particular, the jewels of Albion, running down
The kennels of the streets & lanes as if they were abhorr'd.

The brazed city
reorders its own
destruction, admits
the strutting lords

to the temple,
vandals of sprayed blood —
obliterations
to make their mark.

The spouting head
spiked as prophetic
is ancient news.
Once more the keeper

of the dung-gate
tells his own story;
so too the harlot
of many tears.

Speak now regardless
judges of the hour:
what verdict, what people?
Hem of whose garment?

Whose Jerusalem –
at usance for its bones'
redemption and last
salvo of poppies?

TO THE HIGH COURT OF PARLIAMENT

November 1994
Amos 3:8–11

Keep what in repair?
Or place what further
toll on the cyclic
agony of empire?

Judgement and mourning
come round yet again
like a festival
of scratched heroic film.

I cannot say how
much is still owing
to the merchant house
of Saxe-Coburg-Gotha

from your right ranters,
proud tribunes, place-men,
shape-shifting nabobs,
come the millennium,

judged by the ill-fitted,
the narrow oblong-
sutured, jaws of knee-
puppets jerked to riposte,

by final probate
or by exception –
the voice of Amos
past its own enduring.

PISGAH

I am ashamed and grieve, having seen you then,
those many times, as now

                         you turn to speak
with someone standing deeper in the shade;
or fork a row, or pace to the top end
where the steep garden overlooks the house;
around you the cane loggias, tent-poles, trellises,
the flitter of sweet peas caught in their strings,
the scarlet runners, blossom that seems to burn
an incandescent aura towards evening.
This half-puzzled, awkward surprise is yours;
you cannot hear me or quite make me out.
Formalities preserve us:

                         perhaps I too am a shade.

TO JOHN CONSTABLE: IN ABSENTIA

Eheu! quam tenui e filo pendet
Quidquid in vita maxime arridet.

Anxious griefs, grievous anxieties, are not to be
sublimed through chiaroscuro. Knowing this,
                                    you framed it clearly.
To mourn is to mourn; the ancient words suffice,
Latin or English, worn channels for the rain,
                                    charged and electric.
We suffer commonly, where we are quite alone,
not the real but the actual natures of things;
and there is now, assuredly, no telling
how spirit readied the hand to engineer
a perceptible radiance – arched and spectral –
the abrupt rainbow's errant visitation.

DARK-LAND

Are these last things reduced
to the imagining
of shadow-eternals?
Suddenly in the day's flame

very late he saw it
at Dedham: the English
church as it must be
charred in its own standing,

small, distinct, monochrome,
blazed at from rayed clouds,
rallying to that place,
Sheol if not Shiloh.

MYSTICISM AND DEMOCRACY

i

Ill-conceived, ill-ordained, heart's rhetoric:
hour into hour the iron nib hardly
                              pausing at the well –
inscribed silver, facets of Stourbridge glass,
polished desk surface; the darkling mirrors
                        to an occult terrain:
mystical democracy, ill-gotten, ill-bestowed,
as if, long since, we had cheated them,
                              our rightful, righteous
masters, as though they would pay us back
                              terrific freedoms –
Severn at the flood, streaked pools that are called
                                        flashes
wind-beaten to a louring shine.

ii

Let this not fall imputed to our native
                              obdurate credulities.
Contrariwise within its own doctrine it spins,
remote saturnian orb: oblivious
the imperial granites, braided, bunched, and wreathed;
                              the gilded ornature
ennobling lowly errors – exacted, from exalted –
                        tortuous in their simplicity;
the last unblemished records of service
                              left hanging
in air yellowed with a late half-light
as votive depositions
                        not to be taken down.

EZEKIEL'S WHEEL
i.m. Christopher Okigbo, 1932–1967

I

Consider now the valley
of Hinnom – the trucks
from the abattoir
skidding their loads,
the shameless body parts.
Ezekiel's wheel
shall encompass all:
each flame-warped spirit
dancing unshriven,
the righteous no less
than the jettisoned
gobbets in limbo.
Here too the shrieking
of witness, zealots
high on propane
                  cracked
faces in the smoke.

II

Praise-song for oil drums,
a psalm of spillage:
these things these men
named and unnamed
sold and selfsold
to the generations.
Ezekiel's wheel
shall eternize all
but to no end –
posthumous sodalities
of the traduced
feasting traduction.
Cannot? Why – what
cannot you not think?
Is it that you are cast,
wan ghosts of the ditch,
as in all things equal
unequally gifted
to the wild dog?

III

Summon again the epoch
serving photographers
envoys and rhapsodists
importunate to the sight.
Have them memorize
a blast-furrowed
nameless carrefour
half-way to Jericho
strewn with your rags.
That from old prophecy,
this to lament.
Let the brittle
devourers, the locusts
of pity, enrobe you;
let the veteran
maimed fig tree stand
stark out of the waste.

I V

The scroll is final:
last breath of the ruah
self-quenched in wrath.
Ezekiel's wheel
engenders all
living and dying
even in Christ
and Mary who raised
Christ and is risen with him.
Her migrant accursed
Moabite blood
obscurely pardoned,
at the far limit
for our atonement
still she follows Ruth
gleaning to the last
corner of the worst field
the bane of Judah.

PSALMS OF ASSIZE

I

Hinc vagantur in tenebris misere, quia non credunt veritati ipsi . . .
Querunt lumen confisi ipsis et non inveniunt.

Why should I strike you with my name
why trade impress of proud wounds
come now belated
                              patrons of wrath
anxieties are not rectitudes
holiness itself falls
to unholy rejoicing
to resurrect the dead
myth
        of our salvation
blasphemies no less
mercies
            let us pray
Gabriel descend
as a mood almost
                              a monody
of chloroform
or florists roses
consensual angel spinning his words
                              thread
he descends
            and light
sensitive darkness
                    follows him down

II

Non potest quisquam utrisque servire, simulque ascendere
et descendere; aut ascendas aut descendas oportet . . .

Ascend through declension
the mass the matter
the gross refinement
   gravitas
everlasting obsession
vanity by grace
the starred
       misattributed
works of survival
attributes even now
hallowing consequence
chants of the trace elements
the Elohim
       unearthly music
given to the world
message what message
      doubtless
the Lord knows
when he will find us
     if ever
we shall see him
with the elect
     justified
  to his right hand

III

*Prima actio cultus [dei], ex quo consuetudo
colendi et [mos] religiosus . . .*

Sentences garbled
anger
    indignities
foisted as sorrow
silently acclaimed
in the magisterium
of the lily
    unbroken
the tried and retried
spirit
    the steady
reading of such default
disinheritance also
is inherited
like plenitude
awesome in its way
look provost
for constancy
    the stars
lucent as ardent
as by deeds assigned
to the ephemera
    to our
unending distress

IV

*Hac sola ratione semper eris liber: si volueris
quaecuumque fiunt ita fieri, et omnia in
bonam partem verte.*

Seeing how they stand
with what odds
                    by what rule
of accidence resolved
the irresolute
                    the feats
of hapless jubilo
                    the gifts
set down to derision
rejoice in them
as things that are mourned
loving kindness
                    and mercy
righteousness
patient abiding
and whatever good
is held
        untenable
the entire complex dance
of simple atonement
as in a far fetched
                    comedy
making of sleep and time
timeless healers

V

Collige autoritates et presentia et preterita cerne.

Urbs Sion Mystica
      how comely
the ambient lamps
       impendent
and instruments of brass
        and calloused
labourers at the word
a fine miracle
swung by its ways
       too soon
too soon the fanfare
of visions
     the godly
and noble design
blown to ungoverned
laws of rancour
as freedom dictates
the feast is finished
our cryptic lord of the talents
has left us
     asperged
with lumpen spittle
       amen
say amen as in mammon

VI

*Homini autem nulla umbra sapientie magis
in promptu est quam sua ignorans natura.*

And yet
       the instinctive
salutation
         that now must seem
willed and awkward
we cannot know God
                we cannot
deny his sequestered
power
       in a marred nature
if eloquent at all
           it is
with the inuring of scars
and speechlessness
it does not improve Sion
it has no place
          among psalms
to the chief musician
it goes without lament
          it is not
the almond branch prophetic
            wakefulness
nor is it any kind of blessing
          given this people

VII

Victo carne et sanguine restant demones;
numquam vitabimus. Huc illuc semper adest.

The great O of advent
        cum sibylla
O that nothing may touch
this unapproachable
levity of the creator
conscience and guilt
the formal alchemy
not held to trial
for what is beyond
such mercurial reckoning
its ultimate
                cadence
its fall impeccable
the condign
                salvation
pure carnival in the spirit
                even so
God of miracles the crying
                even so
this is how it ends
how it goes at the last day
                spargens sonum
the day of bitten tongues
say what you like

A SONG OF DEGREES

It is said Adonai your hidden word
declares itself
        even from obscurity
through energies dispersed
        fallen upon stasis
brought by strangers to interpretation,
aspirant to the common plight.

Destined, as natural heirs of the spirit,
your prodigal unholy fools
                raised stones
in deserts; in the temples cast them down;
things past and things to come unshaken
empire of chagrin,
           of the chronically betrayed.

Plight into plight; there you commit your law
to chance
        inescapable witness:
a centurion's cry, the women
bearing their oil or blood; here you release
Bartimeus for ever
          to his blind faith.

OF CONSTANCY AND MEASURE

i.m. Ivor Gurney

One sees again how it goes:
rubble ploughed in and salted
                      the bloods
haphazard fatalities
our scattering selves allowed
their glimpse of restitution –
                    the orchards
of Sarras or Severn bare
plenitude first and last –
as if constancy were in time
given its own for keeping
                    as such gifts belong
to the unfailing burden of the planet
with so much else believed to be fire and air

TO WILLIAM LAW: IN ABSENTIA

To fall asleep in the flesh
is nothing. Resurrection
challenges torment. There is always
the deists' Eden, a measured exile
at home among our mourning cedars.
Looking back, it is you I see stand
quiet, exact, under the tree of conviction –
image to mirage, mirage withdrawing
                    to skeined light,
light to the unmoved miraculous
                      pool of Siloam.

CONCERNING INHERITANCE

It is with civic matters as with some questions
of conventional faith: as with professors of strict
canon who vehemently follow nature,
enthusiasts of sublime emptiness
mountaineering into old age, worshippers
of the unassailable ice-flower:
                         as to prize apologists
for plebeian nobleness, who would have found it hard
telling one servitor from another, who spun
half-crowns to enlightenment – *I take this penny* –
grant inequity from afar to be in equity's covenant,
its paradigm drawn on the fiducial stars,
its aegis anciently a divine shield
                                   over the city.

MYSTICISM AND DEMOCRACY

Great gifts foreclosed on; loss and waste offset
by thrifty oddities of survival –
dittander and black saltwort that are found
.   flourishing on the midland brine.
Flesh has its own spirit, confused with torpor,
deeper than most rooted faiths, deeper than Passchendaele.
Piety is less enduring though it endures much
and with its own stiff diligence keeps the ground
                    set for humiliation.
There was a time, any Methodist could have told you
Ebenezer means stone of help.
                    As for the rest,
ruunt in servitium, crammed vacancy's rabble –
this also is admitted: *introit turba*.

TO THE HIGH COURT OF PARLIAMENT

November 1994

– who could outbalance poised
                Marvell; balk the strength
of Gillray's unrelenting, unreconciling mind;
grandees risen from scavenge; to whom Milton
                addressed his ideal censure:
once more, singular, ill-attended,
staid and bitter Commedia – as she is called –
delivers to your mirth her veiled presence.

None the less amazing: Barry's and Pugin's grand
dark-lantern above the incumbent Thames.
You: as by custom unillumined
                masters of servile counsel.
Who can now speak for despoiled merit,
                the fouled catchments of Demos,
as 'thy' high lamp presides with sovereign
equity, over against us, across this
densely reflective, long-drawn, procession of waters?

ACKNOWLEDGEMENTS

Some of these poems first appeared in *Agenda*, the *Spectator*, the *Sunday Correspondent*, *The Times* and *The Times Literary Supplement*, also in the final section of *New and Collected Poems, 1952–1992*, published in the USA by Houghton Mifflin Company, 1994.

The sources of the various epigraphs used throughout this book are, in order of appearance:

'Mysticism and Democracy' ('You see the terrain ...'): Psalm 118:19 in *The Book of Common Prayer*, 1662.

'Scenes with Harlequins': Avril Pyman, *The Life of Aleksandr Blok*, 2 vols (Oxford University Press, 1979–80), vol. I, p. 275; vol. II, p. 365. By permission of Oxford University Press.

'De Jure Belli ac Pacis': Part II: Ger van Roon, *Neuordnung im Widerstand* (Munich, 1967), p. 155, commenting on a letter of von Haeften, 23 December 1938. A translation of van Roon's book was published in London by Van Nostrand Reinhold Company in 1971 with the title *German Resistance to Hitler: Count von Moltke and the Kreisau Circle*; the corresponding passage can be found there, pp. 54–5. Part VI: An Easter hymn by Martin Luther, '*Christ lag in Todesbanden*', set by J. S. Bach in his Cantata no. 4. Part VIII: *Aufstand des Gewissens: der militarische Widerstand gegen Hitler und das NS-Regime 1933–1945* (Herford & Bonn, 1984), p. 183.

'Sorrel': John Amphlett and Carleton Rea, *The Botany of Worcestershire* (Birmingham, 1909), p. 317.

'Mysticism and Democracy' ('To the Evangelicals ...'): John Bunyan, *The Pilgrim's Progress: The Second Part*. The words are spoken by Valiant-for-Truth.

'Churchill's Funeral': Part I: Jerrold Northrop Moore, *Edward Elgar: A Creative Life* (Oxford University Press, 1984), p. 342, quoting a note by Elgar on the original inspiration for his Overture *Cockaigne*. By permission of Oxford University Press. Part II: John Ruskin, *Unto This Last*, 1862, 'Preface'. Part III: William Blake, *Milton*, 44:34–5. Part V: William Blake, *Jerusalem*, 31:17-18.

'To John Constable: In Absentia': The epitaph placed by John Constable on his wife's tomb in Hampstead churchyard.

'Psalms of Assize': John Colet's marginalia to the *Epistolae* of Marsilio Ficino. See Sears Jayne, *John Colet and Marsilio Ficino* (Oxford University Press, 1963), pp. 87–132. By permission of Oxford University Press.

The title 'Mysticism and Democracy' was suggested by Rufus M. Jones's *Mysticism and Democracy in the English Commonwealth* (New York, 1932), and I have taken the title 'De Jure Belli ac Pacis' from Hugo Grotius (1583–1645).

In 'Cycle' I take 'savage indignation' from W. B. Yeats's 'Swift's Epitaph', which translates Swift's own Latin, '*saeva indignatio*'.

In 'Concerning Inheritance' I allude to an anecdote in William Empson, *The Structure of Complex Words* (Chatto & Windus, 1951), p. 422, concerning a lecture by Bertrand Russell.

Visit Penguin on the Internet
and browse at your leisure

- preview sample extracts of our forthcoming books
- read about your favourite authors
- investigate over 10,000 titles
- enter one of our literary quizzes
- win some fantastic prizes in our competitions
- e-mail us with your comments and book reviews
- instantly order any Penguin book

and masses more!

'To be recommended without reservation ... a rich and rewarding on-line experience' – Internet Magazine

www.penguin.co.uk

READ MORE IN PENGUIN

In every corner of the world, on every subject under the sun, Penguin represents quality and variety – the very best in publishing today.

For complete information about books available from Penguin – including Puffins, Penguin Classics and Arkana – and how to order them, write to us at the appropriate address below. Please note that for copyright reasons the selection of books varies from country to country.

In the United Kingdom: Please write to *Dept. EP, Penguin Books Ltd, Bath Road, Harmondsworth, West Drayton, Middlesex UB7 ODA*

In the United States: Please write to *Consumer Sales, Penguin USA, P.O. Box 999, Dept. 17109, Bergenfield, New Jersey 07621-0120.* VISA and MasterCard holders call 1-800-253-6476 to order Penguin titles

In Canada: Please write to *Penguin Books Canada Ltd, 10 Alcorn Avenue, Suite 300, Toronto, Ontario M4V 3B2*

In Australia: Please write to *Penguin Books Australia Ltd, P.O. Box 257, Ringwood, Victoria 3134*

In New Zealand: Please write to *Penguin Books (NZ) Ltd, Private Bag 102902, North Shore Mail Centre, Auckland 10*

In India: Please write to *Penguin Books India Pvt Ltd, 706 Eros Apartments, 56 Nehru Place, New Delhi 110 019*

In the Netherlands: Please write to *Penguin Books Netherlands bv, Postbus 3507, NL-1001 AH Amsterdam*

In Germany: Please write to *Penguin Books Deutschland GmbH, Metzlerstrasse 26, 60594 Frankfurt am Main*

In Spain: Please write to *Penguin Books S. A., Bravo Murillo 19, 1° B, 28015 Madrid*

In Italy: Please write to *Penguin Italia s.r.l., Via Felice Casati 20, I-20124 Milano*

In France: Please write to *Penguin France S. A., 17 rue Lejeune, F-31000 Toulouse*

In Japan: Please write to *Penguin Books Japan, Ishikiribashi Building, 2-5-4, Suido, Bunkyo-ku, Tokyo 112*

In South Africa: Please write to *Longman Penguin Southern Africa (Pty) Ltd, Private Bag X08, Bertsham 2013*

READ MORE IN PENGUIN

POETRY LIBRARY

Blake	Selected by W. H. Stevenson
Browning	Selected by Daniel Karlin
Burns	Selected by Angus Calder and William Donnelly
Byron	Selected by A. S. B. Glover
Clare	Selected by Geoffrey Summerfield
Coleridge	Selected by Richard Holmes
Donne	Selected by John Hayward
Dryden	Selected by Douglas Grant
Hardy	Selected by David Wright
Housman	Introduced by John Sparrow
Keats	Selected by John Barnard
Kipling	Selected by Craig Raine
Lawrence	Selected by Keith Sagar
Milton	Selected by Laurence D. Lerner
Pope	Selected by Douglas Grant
Rubáiyát of Omar Khayyám	Translated by Edward FitzGerald
Shelley	Selected by Isabel Quigly
Tennyson	Selected by W. E. Williams
Wordsworth	Selected by Nicholas Roe
Yeats	Selected by Timothy Webb

READ MORE IN PENGUIN

A SELECTION OF POETRY

James Fenton Out of Danger

A collection wonderfully open to experience – of foreign places, differences, feelings and languages.

U. A. Fanthorpe Selected Poems

'She is an erudite poet, rich in experience and haunted by the classical past ... fully at home in the world of the turbulent NHS, the decaying academies, and all the draughty corners of the abandoned Welfare State' – *Observer*

Craig Raine Clay. Whereabouts Unknown

'I cannot think of anyone else writing today whose every line is so unfailingly exciting' – *Sunday Times*

Marge Piercy Eight Chambers of the Heart

Marge Piercy's poetry is written to be read and spoken aloud, to move, provoke and entertain, on every subject under the sun from ecology to cats and cookery, to political, sexual and family relationships.

Joseph Brodsky To Urania
Winner of the 1987 Nobel Prize for Literature

Exiled from the Soviet Union in 1972, Joseph Brodsky has been universally acclaimed as the most talented Russian poet of his generation.

Paul Celan Selected Poems
Winner of the first European Translation Prize, 1990

'The English reader can now enter the hermetic universe of a German–Jewish poet who made out of the anguish of his people, things of terror and beauty' – *The Times Literary Supplement*

READ MORE IN PENGUIN

A SELECTION OF POETRY

Octavio Paz Selected Poems

'His poetry allows us to glimpse a different and future place ... liberating and affirming' – *Guardian*

Fernando Pessoa Selected Poems

'I have sought for his shade in those Edwardian cafés in Lisbon which he haunted, for he was Lisbon's Cavafy or Verlaine' – *Sunday Times*

Allen Ginsberg Collected Poems 1947–1985

'Ginsberg is responsible for loosening the breath of American poetry at mid-century' – *New Yorker*

Carol Ann Duffy Selected Poems

'Carol Ann Duffy is one of the freshest and bravest talents to emerge in British poetry – any poetry – for years' – *Independent on Sunday*

John Updike Collected Poems 1953–1993

'Updike's eye comes up very close ... yet eschews the gruesome, keeps life vivid and slippery and erotic' – *Observer*

Frank O'Hara Selected Poems

With his unpremeditated, fresh style, O'Hara broke with the academic traditions of the 1950s and became the life and soul of the New York school of poets.

Dannie Abse Selected Poems

Medicine, music, the myths of Judaism, the cities of London and Cardiff – all recur in poems composed in a spare and witty style.

Penguin Modern Poets

A new series celebrating, in ten volumes, the best and most innovative of today's poetic voices.

READ MORE IN PENGUIN